W9-CAR-884

# Running Upon The Wires

ALSO BY KATE TEMPEST

*Everything Speaks in its Own Way*

*Brand New Ancients*

*Hold Your Own*

*Let Them Eat Chaos*

*Kate Tempest*

# Running Upon The Wires

BLOOMSBURY PUBLISHING
NEW YORK • LONDON • OXFORD • NEW DELHI • SYDNEY

*Much of this book came together while a resident Fellow*
*at Civitella Ranieri.*
*Grateful acknowledgement of their support.*

BLOOMSBURY PUBLISHING
Bloomsbury Publishing Inc.
1385 Broadway, New York, NY 10018, USA

BLOOMSBURY, BLOOMSBURY PUBLISHING, and the Diana logo are
trademarks of Bloomsbury Publishing Plc

First published in 2018 in the United Kingdom by Picador
First published in the United States 2018

Copyright © Kate Tempest, 2018

All rights reserved. No part of this publication may be reproduced or
transmitted in any form or by any means, electronic or mechanical,
including photocopying, recording, or any information storage or retrieval
system, without prior permission in writing from the publishers.

Bloomsbury Publishing Plc does not have any control over, or responsibility
for, any third-party websites referred to or in this book. All internet
addresses given in this book were correct at the time of going to press. The
author and publisher regret any inconvenience caused if addresses have
changed or sites have ceased to exist, but can accept no responsibility for
any such changes.

ISBN: TPB: 978-1-63557-019-9; eBook: 978-1-63557-018-2

Library of Congress Cataloging-in-Publication Data is available

A catalogue record for this book is available from the British Library

2 4 6 8 10 9 7 5 3 1

Printed and bound in the U.S.A. by Berryville Graphics Inc., Berryville,
Virginia

To find out more about our authors and books visit www.bloomsbury.com
and sign up for our newsletters.

Bloomsbury books may be purchased for business or promotional use. For
information on bulk purchases please contact Macmillan Corporate and
Premium Sales Department at specialmarkets@macmillan.com.

'My body was like a harp and her words and gestures were like fingers running upon the wires'

(Joyce, *Dubliners*; p37)

# Contents

*the beginning*

*the end*

# Awake all night thinking of you

Even the rain was quiet
The trees all held their breath
There were no words in any mouth
That were worth being said

Everything was Argument
And everywhere was Rage
Opinion wrung her whittled hands
And settled in her cage

Outside the sky was falling in
Our flesh had come away
We walked around in separate rooms
Looking for the day

The day was gone. My spine was chalk
My mouth, unopened mail
I remembered walking home with you
And I grew pale

      Born in blood
      Born to bleed

      Born for love
      Born by degrees

      Born and Born and Born in you
      Like you were Born in me

*I've been here before*
Said the raindrop to the poisoned sea

The candlelight is small and strange
My face is in the windowpane
Outside the trees are wind-sung poems
The sky's a wound that shows the bone

I was given a loop to trace:
The hook, the hearth, the hill
I was born to be your bed
And I'm born for that still

# Things I do in our house since you left

Come to, breathing
*What am I doing?*
I'm looking for you
but you have gone missing

Who are these people?
Where are the children
I wanted to carry
to make us both women?

What's this I'm holding?
Where is my body?
The floor's made of glue
I can't get it off me

When did the walls
Soften to bruised fruit?
I need to get out more
I can't find my shoes though

I wake in the night and hear noises
I stand on my own by the window
I stare at the door and see faces
I can't hear a word that they're saying

I'm fine, I'm a catch, people tell me
And we were no match
        This is healthy

I eat and I sleep and I stare at my feet
And I'm busy, I'm so busy
Leave me alone
        I'm typing your name in my phone

# Not now but soon

With enough time                              it will be like it never happened
With enough distance                                  our bodies will forget

Waiting for the kettle, suddenly              we'll be drawn backwards
Understanding the unfathomable                    things the other said

# I was a nightmare the whole time I know it

She held my throat and kissed me, slapped me hard across the jaw
I was spinning for her angles up against the toilet door

I've been in a state of shock ever since that kiss
Looking for that cubicle each time I take a piss

We were in the street and I was staring in amazement
At the light against the leaves as they fell towards the pavement

Her face was stretched as taut as the tightrope that we swayed on
As the argument I'd started and then tried to walk away from

# Keeping Busy

I wake up in hotel rooms and fall over on my way to
The shower and put my clothes on inside out
I see the shape of your body in every bare branch
In every cereal bowl and water-jug
The driftwood, the vandalized statue, the train station roof

The whole world is a sick joke about how beautiful you are

# So I moved back to the old neighbourhood

There is sex and mouths up close
To exorcise her holy ghost
The burning of the sweetest parts
Naked rituals in the dark

There is truth, the space between
The way this place has always been
And where it is and where it's not
It's still my place, my weakest spot

The betting shop, the stinking drains
The meat-fridge trucks and dead remains.
The interfaith kids' football games
Shut pubs. New street-food bars. More trains

Pitbull, dogtooth, rib-sick foxes
Memories in cardboard boxes
Out the front wall getting soaked
Bus stop ponced roll-ups half-smoked

Scroll the phone and choose a body
Take me as you want to find me
Space at last, the single life
And nothing in this flat reminds me

Of the way it was with her
Give me this, the grit I know
Meet you in the pub in ten
Then come back here and lay me low

# On finding photographs you took of us

I hear screams from outside the open window and I am shocked to
   remember that other people exist

People are queuing by the cat neutering clinic, as they do at this
   time each morning
Nothing unusual in the long queue of people with their cats in
   boxes,
In line for the desexing offered to residents of the borough.

A cat has got loose from its box
A car has stopped at a green light,
All the people have dropped their boxes
And are in varying states of despair,
Crouching around the car
The cars behind are beeping their horns
And people are shouting

I watch head-scarfed old ladies hold up the traffic while young
   men in impeccable tracksuits crawl on their knees;
School-children in neat braids and white socks and long-haired
   teenage goths and even a couple of dogs are helping.
People are dropping their rucksacks and handbags and lying
   down flat in the road.

I go back to the photographs.
Suntanned topless strangers with our faces.
And there we are together, kissing in that room we stayed in.

The queue has reassembled.
Some people are sitting with their cat boxes between their legs,
 their bums on the pavement, their backs against the clinic wall.
Two women are standing, wearing raincoats, talking to each other
 with their hands.

# Seeing other people

Pushed around on tides of it
her face is close, her eyes are slits
*oh Kate*, she says, I rise to it

We smile like this is something but the gestures
all seem posed. Well aware that morning comes
and finds us separate and closed

We go for drinks, they take me home
the heartthrob I have dreamed of being. Sort of sure
that my heart's lost

and can't bear what it's seeing.

# Headfuck

If I get over you, you might come back
You still love me but you can't promise anything
If I wait for you, nothing will change, I won't do
The work you need me to do
You tell me you think it would be good for me to get involved with
someone else

I go to the pub and stare at the beer taps

# Poem to a barmaid

I stand before you, dumb as mud, breathless at the bar
Turned to chewed-up mush by all the things I know you are

I haven't felt this way for years; you must know it's killing me
All I want to do is be cool, but you've been filling me

With things I haven't dared to hope I'd feel. I try and stop it
But every time you look at me, my eyes fall out my sockets

Pulsate on the floor like hatching pupae at my feet
My body turns to pick-up sticks that fall into a heap

Three drinks in, I gulp, pluck up the courage, try my luck.
Soon as you turn my way, the only word I have is *fuck*

# Three months no contact

I am standing underneath the decorative arch in the hotel gardens, it feels like an experiential theme park ride about the perils of decadence. The fallen rain stills the hum in the air. I have recently discovered I am obsessed with things I don't care about. Cramps in my stomach from *do you think they could tell we'd been fighting?* Waking in the night *did I laugh too loud at the dinner? When will I learn how to dress like an adult?* Yeats had a brown three-piece suit and a monocle, he wanted to become the Eccentric Poet. *He mythologised himself* says the important man talking to me at the important event. I stand under the arch in the tropical opulence ride in the last days of humanity and my Dad is having a pacemaker fitted and staying awake through the procedure and a man with a face like an elbow is talking to a tired waiter saying *I don't want to drink instant coffee I want fresh coffee* and the waiter is smiling without moving his mouth and I care about things like *are you safe? Are you safe? Where are you? Are you safe?*

# Getting out more

I'm inviting
one night stands
To come to gigs
and meet my friends
I don't know
when this will end
I call you up.
It rings
and rings

# A place that meant something to me

I was furtive and shy
as I led you down wet alleys, through broken fencing.
The slime banks of Deptford, the makings of me
I showed you my soul in the rusted old anchor, the smashed-up TV.

The river was wild that night.
Churning and patterned with diamonds and crosses
And I walked with you over the green clay of that beach,
The mudflat by the Thames where I went to get lost.
Beneath the pier that creaked in the squall
And the smell of the city, the sewers, the river.
I watched you quietly
I hoped that you weren't going to laugh.

The wind was as bitter as we have become.

You took your clothes off
Kept your coat on.
You walked towards me
Your naked tits and your eyes and your skin in the rain.

And we fucked standing up, leaning into each other,
In the place that I went to
When I was alone.

Alone again

I've come here today to remember myself,
I'm looking for who used to live in my bones
Before they existed to hope for your kisses.
But London has changed

Even my derelict, secret, wild London
All brown mud and stones,
Has been built over, cleaned up. The rotten old timbers I trod
With my heart in my teeth
Looking down to the black water brawling beneath
Have been wrenched out, replaced

Glass-fronted studios rear up like breakers

# Almost a year and I still can't shake you

I can't be sure that it will ever change
Pulled by something nameless in a song
Standing here before my kitchen window
Feeling you, like you had never gone

As if you might be sleeping in the bedroom
Or somewhere sketching, pins between your lips
Some stupid part still feels you never left me
A part that will not lose the edge it grips

*the middle*

# Aftershowparty

Sat in the plunge of the seeping adrenals
Stage-hot but cooling, drinking for England
And staring intently at whoever's talking
Whole body ringing like cymbals. Or symbols

Show-techs, blue-faced from phones, text home
Somewhere out there they have lives on the boil
But back to the matter of cables to coil
And loitering aimlessly. My body's a drone

A dream of a time, of blossom by water
To walk from my door without chug-sickened A-roads.
But if there was life for me somewhere but here
I'd have found it by now. I get heavy with drink

Eating for boredom. Eating for pleasure.
Sleeping whenever a second comes clear
Head in my arms on the floor of the airport
Probably time for a beer

Get off the internet. Look at the trees in the park
With their leaves in the light like music
Forget that your heart is a piece of brown meat
Feel nothing but love for those that have love

*But if you are a human with a terrifying beauty,*
*Who could make a mess of a mess like me,*

*If everything is music and you like seeing sunrise*
*Getting stoned in bed and staring at the sea —*

Please find me here beside the stage, take me by the floating hands,
lead me to a private place and fuck my heavy brains out

# Heel

I lived at your heel like a dog
I chanted your name and thought you a God
And each time you killed me I liked it
But each part you killed
I forgot

# Firework

The new woman arrived in my life
Like a fire arrives in wet woodland

I was a cave in the dirt
full of claggy old timber

She was the spark

We struggled to take
We couldn't quite catch

But every so often, with enough close attention
Our fire would roar with great authority
And light up the whole sorry place

# A Morning in New Cross

Cooking breakfast in your kitchen I talk nothing
with your housemates
At all times my eyes aware
of how your body moves in baggy clothes

Your shoulders, elbows, legs
emerge from that long shirt
As you brew tea and make us pancakes

I'm scared in case of all the things

I don't think I'm
I don't want to lose again

You shut my brain up with a sweeping hand

# But every soppy fucking song

Careful with the radio
All songs might be the straw

That whips the camel's broken back
And leaves you on the floor

No matter that you've heard the song
Six thousand times before

## I want to be starting something.
## I've got to be starting something

I sleep in our stains. Your shape's in my hands
all day. Transported. The planet's a watch
on the dresser. Dazed in new cities, I'm
with you. I'm close when you want me. It's so good
to miss you. Things that we never expected
to blossom. Reluctant Spring of my love.
Back for a spin. I'm leaving on Sunday.
Life in the space between strangers that stare
at the stage. I keep you warm in my jacket.
I put you on with my socks in the morning.
I kiss my cup when I drink my coffee.

# The First Weekend Away

We Made Love All Day. All Day.
From bedroom to hallway, and outside (the dog needed walking),
And we found the bush by the golf course
And the rain came, nothing could stop us
The rain on our cheeks and the backs of our heads
And my coat laid for the thorns in the grass

Back in the flat, we tried to make food but our love would not let us.
All over that kitchen, and hours,
As we took ourselves deeper inside the other and fed and were fed
And she came inside me and I came inside her and life was created
And she was on top and across and beneath and our legs
Gripped the flood and the tops of the counters and each other's bodies,
And we fumbled for chairs to stand on, to lean over,
Her eyes like two crowns for our heads.

Back in the bedroom, again and still loving.
Unable to stop, to keep bodies from reaching and pulling,
I stroked her skin and was love.
Stoned as the old days. Loving and out of the window
I hear the sea as it roars and submits to itself.

And the next morning, out there, the sun blue bright
The rain stopped for a moment
She shouted and I looked after her pointing hand as she led me
Whispering, out to the beach
There was a rainbow, two rainbows, pouring like waterfalls
From the low cloud into the still sea

She stared at me, small in my arms, huge in my heart,
and her smile was the sky but more mine
and she said *do you see?*

## Hanging out with your friends at the important social occasion

My head is an iron helmet
My throat is bunged with sponge
My nervous system has been hijacked by a team of highly
competitive pop producers

I hope you haven't noticed

I am good manners, very calm,
Nice to be here
Smiling

Truth is

I'm a worm in a fat suit, breathing through a diving bell

# I just need to put some shelves up

Life-hack death-trap
Chicken by the bucketload

Fang-toothed couple
In the B and Q queue

Many-headed phone-face
Automated check out

I recognise the silence
He's me and she's you

Popcorn apocalypse
Shop-floor monotony

It must have been a birthday
We were in a posh hotel

Brimstone screenshot
Quickfix lobotomy

Everything we did seemed to
End in *fucking hell*

Shame-bait advert
Sell-a-dream economy

Knotted up with stress, I broke.
You went to bed

Natural-Look, Easi-Fit,
Self-Adhesive, Master-Lock

Check out robot beeps, I scan
My plank and hang my head

# Moving on, crawling back

It's you again as usual
It was you before we met
And it's still you, despite the fact
That you have long since left

You call me in the evenings
Down the line from far away
We giggle like we used to
There's nothing left that's hard to say

Tonight it's you, as usual,
Creeping round me, speaking low
Keeping me in limbo, dead
To everything I know

You talk about our future
Call me names I've longed to hear
Tell me that you've missed me
I tell you *I had no idea*

We kiss our lovers tenderly
We feel the bliss and burn
But speak when they're asleep
Of all we've yet to learn

# Some days she's everywhere

No one else is us

It's all for show
It's all for show

Marry me again

It's all I know
It's all I know

# This is absolutely normal and nobody is concerned

An elderly man is wearing a large knitted jumper. He stands with
his weight leant forwards and his arms linked behind his back.
His wife, in an upmarket navy blue tracksuit, is being frisked with
a padded electronic swab.

The security attendant is defeating the language barrier by using a
physical display of call and response: first the attendant, then the
elderly lady lift up their legs
and place their feet on to a raised step.

A woman is patiently decanting a bottle of moisturising cream
into smaller containers.

A young couple are holding hands, he with fashion beard and
backwards cap, she with careful smile and sequined jeans. They
stare through Perspex at shelves of dead flesh; the sign behind
them reads *Tender Loving Chicken*

# Venice Beach

The man is power. His board beneath him
leads the wave and in his glory, he tops
a charge more vast and real than daily life

When all our noise has gone and sound becomes
the damp roll and arid hum of air, sea, expanse;
the detritus of life picked to dust, whirling
upwards, the tides will surge undisturbed.
*Trust this*, they say, but the beach ignores
A grey-haired shining woman in a t-shirt
that reads TRUTH HURTS walking group to group
selling Native American dream catchers
and sharpened stick tattoos. *Get yours mama!*
shouts the friendly man in the basketball vest.
They high-five. *Alright!* says a passer-by
nodding, his skin the same texture as the burnt
palms. *Nothing lasts* says the fallen wave

# I don't want to go backwards with her anymore, I want to go forwards with you

I feel you going quiet in my company
I know you're thinking of her. Or thinking of me thinking of her

There's a decoration from our wedding cake
still hanging from the rear-view mirror of my car

Her letters are in my bedside drawer

I take the decoration down and throw it out
I put her letters in a box

My sentences begin – *trust me baby,*
*I've got it all worked out*
At which point I see your eyes
and everything dies
in my mouth

I'm learning to recognise
each pitch in the scale of your silence

# Going forwards with you

Dark of a midnight bedroom
Single flame from the candle in the bowl on the bed-side table
And our skin – red as the night and blue
From the passing sirens
You call a song from my chest

We lie endways after

Through the open window, I watch the dark
Trees and I feel the slow
Wind and the flame is a globe on the wick

You stalk the floorboards, your stomach wrought
Stone as you push your naked breasts into the night

In the morning when I see you, up
Before me, dressing like you're stripping
Wrapped in that tight top, those tiny shorts
You fall into my arms and you fuck me with your shoes on

And as my mouth works around your underwear
I hear myself whispering *I'm yours*
*baby, I'm yours*

*the beginning*

# We went to the river to swim

Angel, you bring everything near
when you caress my forehead
with the bridge of your nose

The droplets of water
that dome on your shoulders
in September sunlight

# At your mother's funeral

Her name carved in stone as if it was someone else's
The right letters, but it had nothing to do with her voice or her temper
or her, running through the flat to open all the windows
so she could listen to the thunderstorm all those storeys up

They tell your wailing grandmother to wait outside and you
walk in to that room alone to watch her burn

Blinking in the sudden light, you pass the anonymous office bungalows
And carefully-kept gravel paths
But stop at the thin stream that runs to the fountain and take off your shoes

One foot in front of the other.
The soles submerged. The sunlight smearing in the heat
A single white feather circles above.
You watch it in silence and gasp when it
lands at your feet

# Duet

Sometimes, when we come together, you scream
like you are being born. I sing like I am dying.

My skin in the morning cool, my feet on
the boards, finding my slippers. Pushing open
the gate of the kettle, for warmth. You are
in bed with a smile on your sleeping mouth.

You play Arabic music, French music,
Madagascan music that I've never heard
I play UK rappers, minimal techno,
Alice Coltrane. Your hair is tied up with
colourful cloth as you move from the hips
through the flat. We cook for each other.
We dedicate days to our lovemaking
Any less than a full day and you look at me, hurt.

I maintain a full wave at my neighbours
But worry about what they hear through the walls –
Aware of how often we wake in the night
and call out for each other

# We bought new sheets

I am telling a story, enjoying myself
I know because my hand is conducting my descriptions
We are driving through golden light
And your body is inclining towards me at all points
As it does when you're happy with me

The lake shines on the watery sun,
the dog sleeps on the bank, one eye watching
as we clutch each other's bodies beneath the darkening mountain
and close our eyes underwater

Night buzzes around us
we shake it till it billows then snap it tight,
pull its edges and fold it under
like a pair of real adults

## But let's not get stale and resentful
## just because we live together

Don't catch me. Falling is all that I want.
In motion I'm better at stillness

God-given strong woman, muscle and form
Churning the dough of the day she makes
Bread and it cooks in the ovens we built to keep warm
She runs the whole world into spinning. Her
Thread unpicks the patterns and she is the morning and
All of the beaches are her golden stomach

And all of the forests are her, and all tree-roots,
And all of the valleys her voice, and all comets

# Dartmoor on Mushrooms

My true love
Came on slowly
Asked for nothing
Till I gave her all
Found myself beside her
In the wood
Beneath
A mighty sprawl
Of moss-bound life
And splendour
Trees as Kings
The river took our skin
And kissed us
Cold and moaning
Blessed our love
And let our love
Begin

# Well

My forehead enjoys the push of her armpit
Her curves are my entire horizon

She makes time a vast plain
Each touch is a portal
To some other place that shudders and
Ticks and extends outwards in waves

The days now are years
All I am concerned with are her breasts

The wetness of her mouth is an ocean I
Sail on or swim through or stare at for peace

There was someone else who lived in this skin before now

I notice how the light regards itself
in the mirror of the pond
but not for long

She is vocal music. Choral.
The rest is canned laughter

# Hormonising

One thing about being two women together is that every single
month we get at least a week when we are both pre-menstrual and
neither of us know what the fuck is going on

# Domestic

Three days into the same row
The last time we kissed without anger is so far away I can't taste it
Shame and reproach

Meanwhile it's Christmas
I made a nut roast

I call my parents to hear all the news
you take this as wargames and sob in the bedroom

I clean the cooker alone

This morning I hear you greeting the dog
as he comes wagging back to the house
And I realise how long it's been
since I last heard you laugh

But when, thank god, the static dries,
the everyday objects lose their menacing aspect
and go back to being curtains or light-bulbs or Tupperware again,

And we can see each other's faces,
our relapse into tenderness
is furious

# Gratitude

I have seen us
Sat together in the evening

Not saying much.
Listening to the fire.

Or laid out on a camping mat,
Your fingertips pulling

At strands of my hair.
Or dancing

To flamenco in the living room.
Well – you dancing.

Me awe-struck, clutching
Your hips.

Your name like a bird
Trying to burst out of my throat

# Love

The way you hold your cup in a closed fist
Your wrists that get rheumatic in the rain
Your long feet, long legs and bony shoulders
Your smile a crash of teeth from nose to chin.

Your eyes drop three octaves when you want me
Your body is transposed into the key
Of sand dunes, raw quartz, heat from a slow sun.
Suddenly as graceful as when you dance
No longer smashing your limbs into
Unmoving table-tops or burning your hands
On every available hot surface
Or head-butting the car door when you dive in

You know, it used to keep me up at night,
The lack of you

# Falling asleep, feeling you falling asleep

So much in a day
and each is
prelude, body, encore

Victor of the last
and victim to
the next

So much left to do
but when I close
the day with you

It's the closest
I have ever come
to rest

# Running upon the wires

Yes, we do repeat. Motifs
occur again, again

This does not mean
we are not new

You are not her.
This is not then.